BEHOLD
THE
GOLFER

Cover Photo ©1995 Superstock, Inc.

Compiled by Mark Rimler

Cover Design by Todd Kelsey

Published by
Great Quotations Publishing Co.,
Glendale Heights, IL

ISBN 1-56245-215-0

Printed in Hong Kong

SECTION I

GOLF TIPS

Swing:
The classic swing is a perfect blending of two elements: The rotational or turning action of the body and the upward and downward hand and arm action.

A player should not assume, once having learned the swing, that this action will be the right one for him to use for the rest of his life.

All you need to do is position your thumbs correctly and you can't help but have a proper grip.

Work from an imaginary
center line that runs down
the top center of the shaft.
Position your left hand so
that the left side of the left
thumb is just to the right of
that center line. Place your
right hand snug on the left
with the right thumb just to
the left of the center line.

To position yourself properly, place your club behind the ball and visualize with your eyes a line from the ball to the pin. Your body should then be parallel to this line and your left shoulder will point to the left of the target.

What you do when and after you hit the ball is far more important than what you do on the takeaway.

Keeping the head still is one of the most challenging tasks. Try this, roll up a sheet of paper, place it in your mouth, point it at the ball and swing. If there is any head movement, the eye will catch it because the pointer will move.

If your are having difficulty turning, check your stance for foot angles.

To cure the overshift, first keep the weight and the middle of your stance at address. Then the proper shoulder turn on the backswing can be easily accomplished. As a result, it becomes virtually impossible to sway.

As you begin the downswing, work on starting the left knee and the hands simultaneously so that the hands and clubhead will arrive at impact together.

When hitting wood shots, there should be no wrist break until after the hands have reached eye level. The hands and arms should continue on through the hitting area in one straight piece.

So for that extra distance, keep the back of the left hand going right out toward the hole until it is at eye level, and keep the hands and arms in one straight piece all the way through the hitting area.

LONG GAME:

Use clubs with extra long shafts. Longer shafts will give you a larger arc and add clubspeed.

If you want to be a longer hitter the answer lies in starting the backswing with the right hip and commencing the downswing with practically simultaneous power action in both feet.

On fairway woods: Do not play the ball in its usual position off the left heel. Move the ball back more than you normally do toward the right foot. Grip the club slightly lower down the shaft in order to shorten your swing and increase your accuracy.

The left heel leads the action
by planting itself firmly on
the ground - which in the
same motion the right heel
comes up off the ground.
Your left hand works with
your left heel and as your
right heel comes up the right
leg straightens, putting the
brake on the right side to
keep from overpowering the
left side.

SHORT GAME:

Every inch you drop from the full length of the grip reduces the shot by 10 yards.

On chipping, first you must ease up on your grip and hold the club as if you were holding a bag of feathers. Second, take the club back with a movement of the hands, arms and shoulders. Knees flexed. On the return to the ball, let the clubhead do the work.

<u>Pitch and run:</u> The weight should be completely on the left foot, hands in front of the clubhead and feet fairly close together - about 4 to 7 inches apart. Keeping the clubface square to the target throughout, remain as quiet as you can on the execution and let the short follow through be stopped naturally by the weight held on the left side and the lack of body action.

<u>Chip shot:</u> The club must be taken back far enough so that you dont stiff arm the shot, and on the return, for good control, the left hand must lead. And lastly, concentrate on the actual hit.

<u>Sand shot:</u> Look at the back of the ball instead of one or two inches behind it. Position the clubbed slightly inside the ball, toward the body, instead of flush center.

Your first move off the ball should be a sharp wrist break. This takes the club up and back outside the line. Next, make a good shoulder turn so the club moves to the inside. This keeps you over the ball and in position to make the shot.

PUTTING:

Your first impression of a
break is the best one. When
you overstudy you become
confused and indecisive.

Get your grip before you step
up to the ball. Don't stand
over it, gripping and
regripping, or you may get so
nervous you cant take the
blade back.

For a straight putt, play the ball on the inside of the left heel. If, however, there is a break in your line, then the ball position should be properly altered. On a left to right break, play the ball to the left toe. On a right to left break, position the ball off the right foot.

On 3 to 7 foot putts: First
put your feet farther apart
than at present. Second,
point your left knee inward
slightly and keep your weight
on the inside of the left foot
with the ball played about
four inches inside the left
heel. Third, on the putt
itself, use an arm stroke
instead of trying to get the
body into the shot.

<u>On long putts:</u> If you are 10 feet from the cup, stroke the ball hard enough to reach 1 foot beyond the cup. If you are 20 feet from the cup, aim for a spot 2 feet behind the hole, and, from 30 feet, stroke it hard enough to go 3 feet past.

CORRECTING A HOOK:

First, keep your head still over the ball. Second, keep your body behind the shot with the right shoulder moving under the chin. And third, strive for a more upright follow-through and a higher arc by driving the left shoulder into a high position.

SECTION II

GOLF QUOTES

If you watch a game it's fun.
If you play it, it's recreation.
If you work at it, it's golf.

> -Unknown

Golf is like a love affair: if you
don't take it seriously, it's no
fun; if you do take it
seriously, it breaks your
heart.

> - Arnold Daly

Action before thought is the ruination of most of your shots.

— Tommy Armour

I've always believed in playing golf for a little something, even if its fifty cents a side.

— Sam Snead

A shot poorly played should be a shot irrevocably lost.

— William C. Fownes

Golf should be a fair test. If
the average golfer shoots 90,
hell be comfortable. If he
shoots 120, hell want to give
up the game.

- Robert Trent Jones

Nothing goes down slower
than a golf handicap.

-Bobby Nichols

Golf is the hardest game in
the world to play and the
easiest to cheat at.

-Dave Hill

I have three-putted in over forty countries.

-Fred Corcoran

It took me seventeen years to get three thousand hits in baseball. I did it in one afternoon on the golf course.

-Hank Aaron

When I first came out on tour, I swung all out on every tee shot. My drives finished so far off line, my pants were grass-stained at the knees.

-Fuzzy Zoeller

Caddies are a breed of their own. If you shoot 66, they say, "Man, we shot sixty-six!" But go out and shoot 77 and they say, "Hell, he shot seventy-seven!"

-Lee Trevino

Golf is an awkward set of bodily contortions designed to produce a graceful result.

-Tommy Armour

Never bet with anyone you meet on the first tee who has a deep suntan, a one-iron in his bag and squinty eyes.

-Dave Marr

Nothing goes down slower
than a golf handicap.
                    -Bobby Nichols

I didn't need to finish college
to know what golf was all
about. All you need to know
is to hit the ball, find it and
hit it again until it disappears
into the hole in the ground.
                    -Fuzzy Zoeller

If you're stupid enough to
whiff, you should be smart
enough to forget it.
                    -Arnold Palmer

Golf is the most fun you can have without taking your clothes off.

-Chi Chi Rodriguez

If I'da cleared the trees and drove the green, it woulda been a great tee shot.

-Sam Snead

Give me a man with big hands, big feet and no brains and I will make a golfer out of him.

-Walter Hagen

Golf is a funny game. It's done much for health, and at the same time has ruined people by robbing them of their peace of mind. Look at me, I'm the healthiest idiot in the world.

-Bob Hope

Every day I try to tell myself this is going to be fun today. I try to put myself in a great frame of mind before I go out then I screw it up with the first shot.

-Johnny Miller

The longer you play, the better chance the better player has of winning.

-Jack Nicklaus

The only time you play great golf is when you are doing everything within your power to lose to your boss.

-Unknown

It was one of those days you dream about. Every hole seemed to be six inches wide.

-Tom Purtzer

Putting isn't golf. Greens
should be treated almost the
same as water hazards: you
land on them, then add two
strokes to your score.
                    -Chi Chi Rodriguez

The only time I talk on a golf
course is to my caddie - and
only then to complain.
                    -Seve Ballesteros

If you keep shooting par at
them, they all crack sooner or
later.

                    -Bobby Jones

The eighteenth,.....one of the great finishing holes in golf.

-Pat Summerall

I've just discovered the great secret of golf. You can't play a really hot game unless you're so miserable that you don't worry over your shots...Look at the top-notchers. Have you ever seen a happy pro?

- P. G. Wodehouse

The way I putted, I must've been reading the greens in Spanish and putting them in English.

-Homero Blancas

Gimme: an agreement between two losers who can't putt.

-Jim Bishop

Most golfers prepare for disaster. A good golfer prepares for success.

-Bob Toski

Golf is the hardest game in the world to play and the easiest to cheat at.

-Dave Hill

A lot of guys who have never
choked have never been in
the position to do so.

-Tom Watson

The golf swing is like sex.
You can't be thinking about
the mechanics of the act
while you're performing.

- Dave Hill

If you travel first class, you
think first class and you're
more likely to play first class.

-Raymond Floyd

It's the most fun I've ever had with my clothes on.

-Lee Trevino

The harder you work, the luckier you get.

-Gary Player

Golf is 90 percent inspiration and 10 percent perspiration.

-Johnny Miller

Golf is based on honesty.
Where else would someone
admit to a seven on an easy
par three?

-Jimmy Demaret

Competitive golf is played
mainly on a five-and-a-half-
inch course, the space
between your ears.

-Bobby Jones

The most difficult lie in golf is
a ball sitting up in the dead
center of the fairway 150
yards from the pin.

-Author Unkown

This may be embarrassing.
I've played in Japan. Is that
anywhere near Asia?

-Fred Couples, when asked
if he had ever played golf
in Asia.

I owe everything to golf.
Where else could a guy with
an IQ like mine make this
much money?

-Hubert Green

That little white ball won't
move until you hit it, and
there's nothing you can do
after it has gone.

-Babe Didrikson Zaharias

I call my sand wedge my half-Nelson, because I can always strangle the opposition with it.

-Byron Nelson

This is the hardest game in the world, believe me. There is no way a golfer can think he is really something, because that's when the game gets you.

-Ben Crenshaw

The average player - if he is lucky - hits six, eight or ten real shots in a round. The rest are good misses.

-Tommy Armour

The golfer who stands at the ball as rigid as a statue usually becomes a monumental failure.

-Dick Aultman

You know you're getting old when you start watching golf on TV and enjoying it.

-Larry Miller

You have to take this game
through so many labyrinths
of the mind, past all the traps
- like, will my masculinity be
threatened if I hit the ball
well and still shoot seventy-
two?

-Mac O'Grady

The good chip is like the good
sand trap shot, it's your
secret weapon. It allows you
to whistle while you walk in
the dark alleys of golf.

-Tommy Bolt

SECTION III

EIGHTEEN PERFECT HOLES

WESTCHESTER COUNTRY CLUB

Harrison, New York

1st hole, 190 yards, par 3

Rather innocuous in appearance, usually described as a "routine" par-three. If you don't have enough club, you land in a bunker in front of the green. Beware, middle handicapper!

MEDINAH COUNTRY CLUB

Medinah, Illinois

No. 3 Course, 2nd Hole, 184 yards par 3

A whole round can be ruined by botching up the second hole of the day. On this 184 yard, par 3 water lies to the left of the second green as well as all the way from the teeing ground to the putting surface. There is a trap on the left side that keeps many a ball from a dip in the pond.

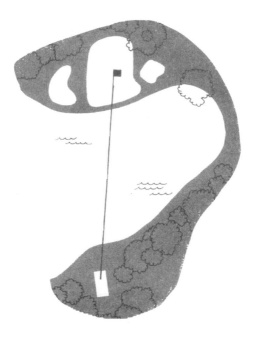

MEDINAH COUNTRY CLUB
No. 3 Course, 2nd Hole, 184 yards par 3

THE NATIONAL

Long Island, New York

Built by Charles Blair Macdonald.

3rd hole, 426 yards par 4

The formidable 3rd hole requires a long accurate tee shot and a blind approach over high dunes.

BANFF SPRINGS

Alberta, Canada

The world famous Devil's Cauldron hole is the 8th on the championship course and the 4th on the Rundle. Picturesque and very difficult, this 171 yard par 3 has an elevated green and water in abundance.

PINEHURST

North Carolina

No. 2 course, the par-5 4th curves gently left on its uphill journey to the green, which is normally reachable in two good shots. The World Golf Hall of Fame is beyond the green.

COLONIAL COUNTRY CLUB

Fort Worth, Texas

5th hole, 459 yards, par 4

The temptation is to play it safe off the tee with a three-wood or one-iron, what with the river flowing so close to the right side and a ditch with over hanging trees on the left edge of the fairway at the landing area where the hole doglegs to the right. But this leaves you with a shot of more than 200 yards to a narrow, two-level green surrounded by bunkers.

PINE VALLEY

Clementon, New Jersey

The "most awesome challenge" at Pine Valley,the 232-yard, par-3 5th where "only God can make a three". The drive carries a wide creek and a belt of scrub to a two-level green.

NCR COUNTRY CLUB

Dayton, Ohio

South Course, 6th hole, 548 yards, par 5

Unless he gets quite wild, the low handicapper should be able to cope with NCR's sixth. Pars and occasional birdies. The middle handicapper ought to get on the green in four occasionally, the high handicapper will be spending time in the ravine in front of the green.

PRINCEVILLE

Kauai, Hawaii

Ocean Nine, 7th hole, 200 yards, par 3

One of the prettiest holes in the world, the ocean is on the right, trees and foliage on the left, mountains in the background, it takes your breath away. It also takes your desire to play away some days when the wind is blowing because you must carry the ocean to reach the green in one.

ROYAL TROON

Scotland

The "Postage Stamp", Troon's famous par 3, 8th hole, at 126 yards is the shortest of all Open Championship holes in Britain. It has seen many holes in one.

WHITEMARSH VALLEY COUNTRY CLUB

Lafayette Hill, Pennsylvania
9th hole, 125 yards, par 3

The short ninth extracts a lot of bogeys, mainly because there is very little margin for error. Trees and out of bounds are close by to the right and at the base of the abrupt slope behind the green.

THE HOMESTEAD

Hot Springs, Virginia

Cascades Course, Upper Course
377 yards, par 4

This tenth hole has a severe dogleg to the right. Along the right side of the fairway from the tee to the landing area is a ravine about a hundred feet deep, full of trees, underbrush, and lost golf balls. The drive is the important shot here.

THE COUNTRY CLUB

Brookline, Massachusetts

Composite Course
11th hole, 445 yards, it is a
demanding par-four with the
green blind from the tee. A
slight draw of the tee shot
down the tree-lined fairway
leaves the player with a long
iron or wood shot across the
pond guarding the entire
front of the green.

THE
COUNTRY CLUB
11th hole, 445
yards, par 4.

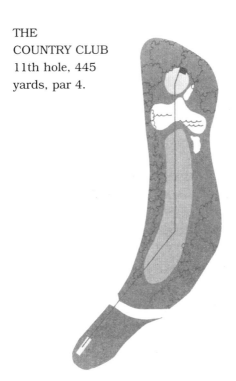

SOUTHERN HILLS COUNTRY CLUB

Tulsa, Oklahoma

12th hole, par 4, 456 yards

The premier golf course in the southwestern section of our country. This hole has a dogleg to the left. The green is also guarded by water front right and side. Three bunkers line the left side of the putting surface. It is imperative that he player stay out of the rough on the right side.

MERION GOLF CLUB

Ardmore, Pennsylvania

East Course, 129 yards, par 3

The 13th at Merion proves that a par-three hole doesn't have to be 230 yards over water to be difficult. The shot is a nine-iron onto a concave green, superbly trapped. If you hit the ball too hard, you are in the big back trap. Hit it too easy and you are in the sand in front. This is bad for the morale on a hole like this.

PINE VALLEY

Clementon, New Jersey

Designed by George Crump
with Henry Colt

The 14th, at 184 yards, is the
last of Pine Valley's gorgeous
short holes. With 50 feet of
water and bunkering fronting
the green, and more water at
the back left, it demands rare
confidence and precision from
the tee.

AUGUSTA NATIONAL

Augusta, Georgia

Designed by Bobby Jones
and Dr. Alister Mackenzie

The beautiful manicured and
fast greens of the par 5 on
the 15th. With water to carry
on the second shot this 500
yards is a formidable hole,
but reachable in two for the
long hitters.

PEBBLE BEACH

Pebble Beach, California.

Designed by Alister Mackenzie

The heart stopping 400 yards, par 3 on the 16th at Cypress Point - play safe to the left, or go for it over the rocks on the right.

BAY HILL CLUB

Orlando, Florida

17th hole, 223 yards, par 3
The 17th is a full carry over
the water, with a long,
shallow trap guarding the
front right two thirds of the
green. Bunkers are also
placed to the left and back of
the green. The green is wide
and shallow, with the
toughest pin placements on
the right side behind the
water and trap.

OLYMPIC

San Francisco, California

Designed by Willie Watson
and Sam Whitey

On the approach to the 18th,
(338 yards, par 4) the shot to
the tiny green has to run the
gauntlet of four bunkers.

19th HOLE NOTES:

Other Hardcovers by Great Quotations

Ancient Echoes
Behold The Golfer
Bumps in the Road
Chosen Words
Good Lies for Ladies
Great Quotes from
    Great Teachers
Great Women
Just Between Friends
Love Streams

The Essence of Music
The Perfect Brew
The Power of Inspiration
There's No Place Like
    Home
To A Very Special
    Husband
Woman to Woman
Works of Heart

Other Titles by Great Quotations

365 Reasons to Eat
    Chocolate
A Smile Increases Your
    Face Value
Aged To Perfection
Apple A Day
Champion Quotes
Close to Home
Don't Deliberate . . .
    Litigate
Each Day A New
    Beginning
For Mother–A Bouquet of
    Sentiments
Golf Humor
Good Living
I Think My Teacher
    Sleeps At School
Inspirations
Interior Design for Idiots

Money For Nothing
    Tips for Free
Mrs. Murphy's Laws
Mrs. Webster's
    Dictionary
Parenting 101
Quick Tips for Home
    Improvement
Quotes From Great
    Women
Real Estate Agents and
    Their Dirty Little Tricks
Teachers Are First Class
The Dog Ate My Car
    Keys
The Secret Language
    of Men
The Secret Language of
    Women
Thinking of You
What To Tell Children

GREAT QUOTATIONS PUBLISHING
1967 Quincy Court
Glendale Heights, IL 60139-2045
Phone (708) 582-2800, Fax (708) 582-2813